JUDGMENT BUT HOPE

Isaiah Part 1

ISAIAH—"The Holy One of Israel"

You're about to study the crown jewel of Old Testament prophets, a book that will fill you with awe as you come face to face with "the Holy One of Israel"—a phrase Isaiah repeats 25 times but which is found only 6 more times in the Bible and only in the Old Testament: once in Kings, three times in the Psalms, and twice in Jeremiah.

God's holiness is a recurring theme. Between 739 B.C. and 681 B.C., Isaiah watched the spiritual and moral deterioration of the Southern Kingdom of Judah and preached the "vision" he received during the reigns of Uzziah Jotham, Ahaz, and Hezekiah (Isaiah 1:1) and likely continued to preach it for part of Manasseh's rule (697-642 B.C.)—possibly the most wicked king of Judah. He knew that no matter how bad things got, Jehovah would ultimately humiliate sin and exalt justice and righteousness. He warns God's people of approaching captivity and the surrounding nations of approaching judgments. But beyond judgment he always looked to the hope of the coming Messiah, His universal kingdom (from sea to sea), justice and restoration!

Jesus quotes Isaiah extensively and Isaiah's name is mentioned 22 times in the New Testament, all associated with prophecies of the Messiah's comings. This program (Part 1) will carry us through the first section of the book (39 chapters). Just as the Bible divides into 39 books of the Old Testament and 27 of the New, Isaiah divides into two sections of 39 chapters and 27 chapters.

There couldn't be a more relevant time to study Isaiah. We're living in identical times—apostasy from the true faith and consequent idolatry of one sort or another, disrespect for justice and the sanctity of human life and marriage, and nations rising up against nations.

We don't know how all this is going to shake out for our nation or any other, but we do know we're reliving Isaiah's times and God wants us to relive his ministry. Like Isaiah, we can trust that the Holy One of Israel will continue to judge sin and promote His love and justice. And we can look to the Messiah's second coming. It's an awesome and exciting time to live in Beloved, a time for us to speak the prophetic Word of God to everyone we know! The message is the same—approaching judgment or salvation.

You'll see this every day as you join with us to learn the book of Isaiah. May the Lord richly bless you in this inductive study!

Kay

PRECEPTS FOR LIFE™
Study Guide

This Bible study material was designed for use with the TV and Radio teaching program, Precepts for Life™ with renowned Bible study teacher Kay Arthur, a production of Precept Ministries International. This inductive 30-minute daily Bible study program airs on many satellite, cable, and broadcast stations, and on the internet at **www.preceptsforlife.com.**

As with all Inductive Bible studies, the best way to use the material is to complete the assignments in each lesson before listening or watching the PFL program for that day. These programs are also available on DVD and CD at **www.preceptsforlife.com** or by phone (1.800.763.1990 for television viewers or 1.800.734.7707 for radio listeners). For more information about the Precept Inductive Bible Study Method and Precept Ministries International, visit **www.preceptsforlife.com.**

These materials are also useful for Bible study apart from the Precepts for Life™ programs. We hope you'll find them valuable for studying God's Word and that your walk will be strengthened by the life-changing Truth you'll encounter each day.

Isaiah Part 1: Judgment—But Hope STUDY GUIDE
Published by Precept Ministries of Reach Out, Inc.
P. O. Box 182218
Chattanooga, TN 37422

ISBN–13: 978-1-62119-000-4

PROGRAM 1 — Listen! The Lord Has Spoken!

TODAY'S TEXT
Isaiah 1:1-4

CROSS-REFERENCES

Isaiah 45:5

Exodus 4:22

Deuteronomy 28:1-2, 15, 20

Psalms 46:10; 119:104

John 1:11-12

1. Read Isaiah 1:1-4, asking the 5 W and H questions (who, what, when, where, why, and how) to determine the context. What do you learn about Isaiah and when he delivers his message? Who does his vision concern?

2. Who is speaking in verse 2? What is He talking about?

3. What do you learn about Israel from these verses? List everything this nation has done to God.

4. Now consider Israel's relationship to God as "son" (Exodus 4:22) and how this relates to you. According to John 1:11-12, who are God's children?

5. Have you, like Israel, rebelled and turned away from God? Are you weighed down with judgments on your bad choices?

PROGRAM 2 — Sin's Painful Consequences

TODAY'S TEXT
Isaiah 1:1-6

CROSS-REFERENCES

Isaiah 45:5

Genesis 15:9-21

Exodus 4:22-23; 6:2-7

Psalm 38:3-9

Romans 1:16; 9:3-5

Philippians 2:10-11, 3:4-6

1. Read Isaiah 1:1-6. Once again note who is speaking, to whom, and when. What has Israel done?

2. How is God described in these verses?

3. What do you learn about Israel's sin from the question posed in verse 5? Who has "stricken" Israel for their rebellion?

4. Now read Romans 1:16 and 9:3-5. What special privileges did God grant Israel?

5. If God remembers His covenant and wants to redeem His people, what can you conclude with respect to yourself? Can anything prevent Him from fulfilling His promises?

PROGRAM 3 — "Come now, and let us reason together"

TODAY'S TEXT
Isaiah 1:2, 3, 7-28

CROSS-REFERENCES
Genesis 18:20; 19:4
**Psalms 51:4, 7, 12;
139:7-12**
Romans 8:17
Galatians 4:7
Hebrews 13:4
1 John 1:9

1. Today let's analyze Isaiah 1:2-3, 7-28, focusing particularly on what the Lord says to Israel. Look for imperatives (instructions/commands) and propositions (declarative sentences) that give you insight into God's character.

2. How is Israel's land described in this chapter? What is happening? (Note: "daughter of Zion" and "faithful city" are synonyms for Jerusalem.)

3. How is Israel's spiritual condition further described in these verses? What do "Sodom" and "Gomorrah" imply?"

4. What must Israel do to be cleansed of their sin (1:18-19, 27)?

5. What will happen if they do not obey the Lord (1:20, 28)?

6. What do you learn about God from these verses? Why does He leave survivors in Israel? How does He deal with sin and with repentance?

PROGRAM 4 — In the Last Days...

TODAY'S TEXT
Isaiah 1:24-31; 2:1-5

CROSS-REFERENCES
Isaiah 1:2, 4, 18, 21
2 Kings 19:22
**Psalm 25:4; 71:22; 78:41;
89:18; 119:105; 135:18**
Jeremiah 50:29; 51:5
Daniel 11:32
Mark 9:44
Luke 13:3
John 8:32, 44
Romans 15:3
1 Corinthians 10:11
Ephesians 5:26
Hebrews 1:2
1 Peter 1:23; 5:8
Revelation 20:10

1. Read Isaiah 1:24-31 and 2:1-5. As you observe the text, mark the following key words:
   a. *Repentant* and (synonym) return with a red U-turn symbol
   b. Time phrases with a green clock (e.g. *then, when, last days,* etc.)
   c. *Jerusalem* (city of righteousness, faithful city, mountain, Zion) with a blue Star of David
   d. *Nations* with a brown underline, shaded green

   > Marking repeated key words and phrases helps unlock the meaning of a text. It slows you down so you can focus on the text then afterward it enables you to quickly compile a list of facts or terms from a chapter. Always ask the 5W and H questions while marking to understand what you're marking.
   >
   > Because you will mark some words throughout your study, consider creating a bookmark with a list of these "keys" and their respective markings.

2. What is God going to do to His "adversaries" according to 1:24-25? Based on prior verses, who does this group include?
3. During this judgment, what will happen in Jerusalem to the:
   a. repentant?
   b. sinners?
4. What will burn and for how long? What does this tell you about the things the world values?
5. What will occur in the last days according to chapter 2? What did you learn from marking nations?

PROGRAM 5 — The Day of Reckoning

1. Read Isaiah 2:1-21 and mark **nation(s)**, **mountain (Jerusalem, Zion)**, and time phrases (**in that day, the day of reckoning,** etc.). How is the Lord described in these verses?

2. Briefly summarize the main points of the last days described in verses 1-4.

3. What does Isaiah call for in verse 5? Why is this also an appeal to Christians today?

4. What happens "in that day," the "day of reckoning?"

5. How should you respond to the truths about the day of the Lord?

PROGRAM 6

Consent and Obey

TODAY'S TEXT
Isaiah 1:2-5, 19; 2:2

CROSS-REFERENCES

Numbers 15:30-31

Deuteronomy 7:6-11

Jeremiah 29:11

Hebrews 12:1, 5-6

1 Peter 1:1-2, 14-16; 4:17

1. In Isaiah 1:2 God calls Israel "sons." Read Deuteronomy 7:6-11. Note the basis on which God chose Israel and for what purpose.
   a. What do you learn about God from this passage?
   b. What was Israel "redeemed" from?
   c. According to verse 11, what is Israel's responsibility?
   d. What does "to a thousandth generation" mean?

2. Review what you learned about Israel's condition in Isaiah 1:2-5. What had they done and how did God strike them according to verse 5?

3. What does God ask them to do in Isaiah 1:19?

4. Read Hebrews 12:1, 5-11 and again note the believer's responsibility. How does God deal with His "sons" and why?

5. Are you living according to God's precepts for life? Is your standard God's standard—holiness?

PROGRAM 7

Woe to the Proud

TODAY'S TEXT
Isaiah 3:1-9

CROSS-REFERENCES

Isaiah 1:1-2; 2:1-6, 12-18, 22

1 Kings 18:21

Psalms 2:4-9; 146:3-7

Matthew 6:24

Mark 16:19

Galatians 1:10

Revelation 19:11-16

1. To get into context for today's study, review Isaiah 2:12-22 to consider who the Lord humiliates.

2. What can you conclude from 2:22 about how society regarded these men?

3. Now read Isaiah 3:1-9, marking references to Jerusalem and the new key word woe with a red cloud shaded brown.

4. Who are the leaders in Jerusalem and what's going to happen to them? Who will rule in their place?

5. Who is leading your country and where to? What criterion determines who you support—popular opinion or God's law?

PROGRAM 8 — The Lord Enters Into Judgment

TODAY'S TEXT
Isaiah 3:1-4:1

CROSS-REFERENCES
Exodus 22:21
Hebrews 13:4

1. Observe Isaiah 3:1-4:1, marking key words including *judge* with a red "J" and *My people* in a distinct way. Review why God is judging Israel's leaders.

2. How are judgments on the righteous and the wicked contrasted in verses 10-11? How does this encourage you to stand for the Lord?

3. What did you learn from marking My people? How are leaders described? What have they done to the people?

4. What ideas and behaviors do people admire in today's leaders (politicians, celebrities, reporters)?

PROGRAM 9 — Life or Judgment?

TODAY'S TEXT
Isaiah 4:1-6; 5:1-7

CROSS-REFERENCES
Isaiah 3:16-26
Leviticus 11:44
Psalm 18:28; 36:9
Lamentations 1:1-3
Ezekiel 16:46-50
John 1:1, 14
Romans 6:23
2 Corinthians 5:21
1 Timothy 2:9-10
Hebrews 4:15

1. Re-read Isaiah 3:16-4:1. Summarize the conduct and appearance of the women and how they will be judged.

2. How do women's standards and choices influence the moral path of society today?

3. Now read Isaiah 4:2-5:7 and mark key words. Mark *survivors of Israel* and its synonyms and add it to your key-word list. (Don't miss references like *he who is left, remnant, everyone who is recorded for life in Jerusalem*.)

4. What did you learn from marking survivors?

5. How will God cleanse Jerusalem? What will Zion look like?

PROGRAM 10 — Woe to the Wicked!

TODAY'S TEXT
Isaiah 5:1-25

CROSS-REFERENCES
Psalm 119:104

Jeremiah 46:11

Daniel 11:32

Hosea 4:1-6

John 8:32

Ephesians 5:16

1. Observe Isaiah 5:1-25, marking key words and asking 5W and H questions. Mark *woe* with a red cloud shaded brown and ***therefore*** with three red dots like a triangle to discover the conclusion the speaker is making. Also identify and mark *well-beloved.*

2. Why does the well-beloved let His vineyard be trampled?

3. What behavior does the first woe address (v.8)? What happens to those who sin this way?

4. What behavior does the second woe address (v.11)? What do these people ignore?

5. What do you learn from the final four woes given in verses 18-23?

PROGRAM 11 | God's Presence in You

TODAY'S TEXT
Isaiah 2:8-12, 17, 22; 3:8

CROSS-REFERENCES
Isaiah 1:1; 42:8

Exodus 19:1-6

Leviticus 26:14-19

Deuteronomy 8:11-14

John 15:16

Acts 17:28

Romans 15:4

1 Corinthians 6:19

Colossians 3:5

Hebrews 13:5-6

1 Peter 1:16

Revelation 1:6

1. Compare God's calling Israel with His calling the Church. Look up the following verses. Note who chooses, who's chosen, when, why (for what purpose), what the elect are freed from and how they live subsequently.
   a. Exodus 19:3-6
   b. John 15:16
   c. Revelation 1:6
   d. 1 Peter 1:15-16

2. In the wilderness Israel lived in the very presence of God – a cloud by day and fire by night. Read Leviticus 26:14-19 and discuss the relationship of pride to disobedience.

3. A key repeated word in Isaiah is *pride*—mark it (including synonyms) with a red arrow pointing up. Also mark references to being *humbled* with an arrow pointing down.
   a. Isaiah 2:8-17
   b. Isaiah 5:15

4. Do you realize that believers live in the presence of God (1 Corinthians 6:19)? Do people see God in your life by the way you act, talk, live, and treat others?

PROGRAM 12 | Becoming God-Conscious

TODAY'S TEXT
Isaiah 3:8-11, 16; 4:2-5

CROSS-REFERENCES
Exodus 13:21-22; 40:17, 19, 29, 34-38

1 Samuel 4:21

1 Kings 8:10-11

Ezekiel 10:1-5, 18-19; 11:22-23; 43:1-4

Romans 8:4

1 Corinthians 6:19

Ephesians 4:30

Philippians 2:15

Hebrews 13:5-6

1 Thessalonians 5:19

1. Today we'll observe God's presence among His people in several cross-references. Cross-references aid interpretation since God rarely says everything about a subject in one place.
   Look up Exodus 13:21-22. How did God lead Israel out of Egypt?

2. Now read Exodus 40:17-38 and mark the key phrase *just as the Lord had commanded Moses.* List everything you learn about the cloud of the Lord.

3. Describe God's presence when Solomon moved the Ark of the Covenant to the newly built temple in 1 Kings 8:10-11.

4. Review Isaiah 3:8-11. Why did God's presence ultimately depart from Israel?

5. Read Ephesians 4:30 and 1 Thessalonians 5:19. If a believer's body is God's temple and dwelling place (1 Corinthians 6:19), how should believers live?

PROGRAM 13 — The Holiness of God

TODAY'S TEXT
Isaiah 5:24-30; 6:1-8

CROSS-REFERENCES
Leviticus 6:9, 12-13; 26:18
2 Chronicles 26:1, 3-5, 15-20
Joel 3:10
Matthew 12:34
1 Corinthians 10:12

1. Read Isaiah 5:24-30, marking key words and the phrase ***distant nation*** and its pronouns (it, its).

2. Why is the Lord angry with His people and how will He judge them (vv. 24-25)?

3. Who will raise up the *distant nation* to judge Israel? How is it described?

4. Now read Isaiah 6:1-8, marking time phrases with a green clock. (Although Scripture frequently uses time units, also look for words that specify event order like "then," "until," "after this," and "when".)

5. When did this event occur? What did Isaiah witness?

6. How did he react to God's holiness? How was he helped?

7. Is the Lord prompting you to respond in any particular way to this program? If so, go humbly before Him now and submit to His will.

PROGRAM 14 — The Richness of His Glory

TODAY'S TEXT
Isaiah 6:1-10

CROSS-REFERENCES
Genesis 1:2, 26; 11:6-7
2 Chronicles 26:18
Proverbs 30:1-4
Matthew 3:17
John 1:1-2; 2:4; 12:27-28, 35-41; 13:9; 14:9
Revelation 13:8

1. Read Isaiah 6:1-10, reviewing your observations from the previous program. Summarize Isaiah's vision.

2. Contrast King Uzziah's (2 Chronicles 26:16-20) and Isaiah's reactions to coming into God's presence. How did God respond to each of them?

3. What does God ask in Isaiah 6:8? What does He tell Isaiah to say?

4. How will people respond to His message?

5. Now read John 12:27-28 and 35-45. Why does the author quote from Isaiah? Why did some people reject Jesus? (What did they reject?)

PROGRAM 15 | When the Word Falls on Deaf Ears

TODAY'S TEXT
Isaiah 6:8-13

CROSS-REFERENCES

Isaiah 1:4, 11-13; 4:4; 5:13

Jonah 2:9

Matthew 7:14, 18-22; 28:19-20

Mark 4:3-12

Luke 2:22; 19:41

John 1:14

Acts 26:8

1 Corinthians 6:19

1 John 3:1

1. Read Isaiah 6:8-13 and mark time phrases and references to *the land.* How long did God tell Isaiah to preach His message?

2. What kind of judgment did Israel face? Review Isaiah 5:13 and 26-30.

3. What hope is offered in 6:13? In light of Isaiah's commission, do you think this encouraged him to persevere?

4. What does Matthew 7:13 and 21 teach about those who enter the kingdom of heaven? What do all true disciples ultimately do?

Let us hear from you!

Have you been blessed by the teachings on *Precepts For Life™?* We'd love to hear your story.

Visit www.PreceptsForLife.com and click "Contact Us." Or write to:

Precepts For Life
P. O. Box 182218
Chattanooga, TN 37422.

Make sure to mention the call letters of the station where you tune in.

PROGRAM 16 — Steadfast and Immovable

TODAY'S TEXT
Isaiah 7:1-9

CROSS-REFERENCES
Ezra 4:10
Isaiah 2:22
Jeremiah 1:12; 13:11
1 Corinthians 15:58
Hebrews 11:6

1. Read Isaiah 7:1-9, asking the 5 W and H questions. Note who's involved, what's happening and where. Mark time phrases with a green clock.

2. Why is the king fearful? How are he and his people described?

3. What does God tell Isaiah to do? What's his message?

4. What does Isaiah warn the king about in verse 9?

5. What do you learn about God's sovereignty from this passage?

PROGRAM 17 — A Sign for Deliverance

TODAY'S TEXT
Isaiah 7:1-14

CROSS-REFERENCES
Isaiah 6:1
Deuteronomy 24:1
2 Chronicles 26:19-21
Matthew 1:18-25
Luke 2:49, 52
John 16:8
Romans 5:12
1 Corinthians 10:12
2 Corinthians 5:21
2 Kings 15, 16 and 17

1. Review Isaiah 7:1-9 noting main characters, then read 2 Kings 15:23-31, 37 and 16:1-5. What do you learn about each king and especially their relationship to God?

2. Who sent Rezin and Pekah against Judah? What did Ahaz do that deserved God's judgment?

3. Now read Isaiah 7:10-14. What does God tell Ahaz to ask for? In light of your observations of Ahaz's character, does his response to this seem genuine?

4. Who is "Immanuel?" (Mark **Immanuel** in a distinct way and add it to your list of key words.) Read Matthew 1:18-25 and list your observations about Him.

PROGRAM 18 — Wait on the Lord

TODAY'S TEXT
Isaiah 7:9, 14-25; 8:1-8

CROSS-REFERENCES
Isaiah 2:22; 6:1-13
2 Kings 15:29; 16:9
Habakkuk 2:4
Romans 1:16-17; 10:17

1. Review God's plan to deliver Judah and His warning to Ahaz in Isaiah 7:3-9. Then read Isaiah 7:14-25 and 8:1-8, marking time phrases and geographical locations.

2. Who did Ahaz trust for deliverance (2 Kings 16:7)? Go back and mark references to *Assyria* in orange in Isaiah chapters 7-8.

3. What did Isaiah prophesy about this alliance?

4. Describe Israel's conditions during Assyria's captivity.

5. Although Ahaz's plan seemed to bring victory to his people, what did his rejection of God's plan result in? Can you see any parallels in your life? Are you suffering consequences from following your own paths? Have they brought pain and hardship on others as well?

PROGRAM 19 — A Spring of Living Waters

TODAY'S TEXT
Isaiah 8:6-14

CROSS-REFERENCES
Isaiah 6:1-8, 13; 7:3, 9,14, 20; 8:1
Psalms 12:6; 119:104
Jeremiah 2:13-19
Acts 20:29
Ephesians 4:14

1. What was Daniel's interpretation of the "handwriting on the wall" (5:24-28)?

2. When did the prophetic words begin to come to pass? What happened?

3. Who replaced Belshazzar? What nationality was he? How old was he?

4. How does this kingdom fit into the dream of the statue in chapter 2?

PROGRAM 20 | Light in Darkness

TODAY'S TEXT
Isaiah 8:11-22; 9:1-2, 6

CROSS-REFERENCES
Isaiah 2:22; 6:13; 7:3, 9, 14; 8:1

Proverbs 23:7

Amos 3:6

Zechariah 13:7

Luke 2:25-32

John 8:12; 17:17

Romans 12:2

2 Peter 1:4; 3:3-9, 11-14

1. Read Isaiah 8:11-22 and 9:1-2, 6, asking the 5 W and H questions. Also mark *testimony* and law with a purple book, shaded green.

2. How does God want Isaiah to walk among "this people" and regard Him?

3. Recall the political climate and spiritual conditions of Israel at this time. Why will the Lord be a snare and trap for them?

4. Who will Isaiah and his disciples wait for?

5. What did you learn from marking testimony and law? How can you know if you're hearing truth?

6. What is the hope for those in darkness—what will they see and where? What do you learn about the coming ruler in 9:6?

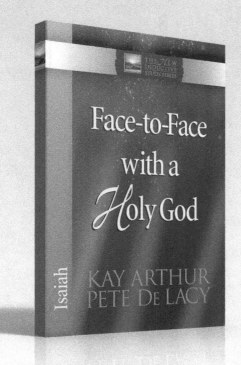

Take your study of end times to the next level.

Discover how you, like Isaiah, can stand strong in the face of attack, persevere in a faithful walk with God, and claim the tremendous promises He has provided. Learn to observe and interpret the prophet's message and apply it to your life.

13-week Study. Six days of guided lessons, 20 to 30 minutes long, help and teach you how to discover God's precepts, purposes and promises on your own.

NEW INDUCTIVE STUDY SERIES
Face-to-Face with a Holy God
(ISAIAH)

www.preceptsforlife.com
ONLINE

1.800.763.1990
TELEVISION

1.888.734.7707
RADIO

PROGRAM 21 — A Sign of Hope

TODAY'S TEXT
Isaiah 9:6-7

CROSS-REFERENCES

Isaiah 5:13; 7:2, 6, 9-14; 10:20-22; 11:1, 10

Exodus 3:14-15

2 Samuel 7:8-16

Psalms 119:104

Matthew 1:18-25

John 8:24

Romans 5:12

2 Corinthians 5:21

Ephesians 6:4

Colossians 2:13-14

Hebrews 11:6

1. Read Isaiah 7:14 (10-14 for context) and 9:6-7. Mark *sign* with an orange stop sign shaded yellow and *child* with a purple circle shaded yellow.

2. What *sign* will God give? What does His name mean?

3. What did you learn about this *child?* What will He do? For how long?

4. How is this *sign* a fulfillment of God's promise to David? Look up Matthew 1:1, 18-25 and note the lineage.

5. Who will the child "govern?" Read Isaiah 10:20-22, 11:10, and Romans 9:24-27.

PROGRAM 22 — A Great Light to Those in Darkness

TODAY'S TEXT
Isaiah 9:1-7

CROSS-REFERENCES

Isaiah 7:9, 14; 8:13-14, 16, 19-22; 9:1-7

Matthew 4:12-17; 11:28-30

John 1:4, 9; 3:3, 5, 16-20; 9:5

Romans 8:37

1. Read Isaiah 8:19-22 and 9:1-7 in one sitting to learn how the chapters connect. How are the people described?

2. What will happen in the regions listed in verse 1? Who fulfills this prophecy according to Matthew 4:12-17?

3. What will God do for those who walk in darkness (9:2-5)?

4. Look up John 1:4, 9; 3:16-20, and 9:5. Who is the light and what do you learn about Him? Who rejects the light and why?

PROGRAM 23 | His Righteous Anger

TODAY'S TEXT
Isaiah 9:5-19

CROSS-REFERENCES

Isaiah 7:9, 25; 8:6-9

Ezekiel 13:9

Jeremiah 14:14

Luke 9:23

Mark 4:31-32

Galatians 2:20; 3:28-29

1. Read Isaiah 9:5-21, marking key words from your bookmark. Also mark:
   a. *righteousness* with a blue R
   b. *therefore* with three red dots like a triangle
   c. *in spite of all this, His anger* with a red cloud, colored yellow
   d. *pride* with a brown arrow pointing up
   e. *time phrases*
   f. *geographical locations*

2. Note the subject shift in verse 8. Who's God warning now?

3. Examine each place you marked therefore. How do the people respond to God's judgment in verses 9-10? Verse 13? Verses 18-21?

4. Who will God cut off? Why? Compare this with Jeremiah 14:14.

5. How does the imagery in verses 18-21 describe the wickedness in Israel? What are they doing to one another and who are they against?

PROGRAM 24 | An Outstretched Hand

TODAY'S TEXT
Isaiah 10:1-33; 11:1

CROSS-REFERENCES

**Isaiah 2:22; 5:24-25;
6:9-13; 7:3, 14; 9:6, 19-21**

Hebrews 12:6-11

1. Read Isaiah 10, marking key words from your bookmark and time phrases. Then carefully re-read the chapter, marking *Assyria* in orange and *remnant* in a distinct way. Include pronouns.

2. Who does God speak the first *woe* to in verse 1 and why? What does He warn them about?

3. What do you learn about Assyria in verses 5-6? What does this teach you about God's judgments?

4. What is Assyria's intention in oppressing Jerusalem? (v.7) How does Assyria's motive compare with God's?

5. What will the Lord do to Assyria when He finishes judging Jerusalem?

6. Who does Assyria credit its victories to? How will God humble their pride?

PROGRAM 25 — A Shoot from Jesse

TODAY'S TEXT
Isaiah 11:1-16; 12:1-6

CROSS-REFERENCES

Isaiah 5:13; 6:13, 7:9, 14; 9:6-7

Genesis 3:15; 49:10

Hosea 4:6

Zechariah 13:8-9

Matthew 24:31

John 1:3; 14:17, 20

Hebrews 4:9-10

Revelation 1:8; 19:15-16; 22:16-17

1. Today we'll conclude the second segment of Isaiah (chapters 7-12). Read Isaiah 11:1-16 and 12:1-6, marking key words from your bookmark. Note everything you learn from marking the following:
   a. *Knowledge* (dark green)
   b. *Righteousness* (blue R)
   c. *Then* (green circle)
   d. Time phrases like in *that day*
   e. *Remnant*
   f. *Salvation* (with a large S)
   g. Geographical locations including *in all the earth*

2. How is the Messiah described in Isaiah 11:1-5? What do you learn about His righteousness?

3. Compare Isaiah 11:4 with Revelation 19:15-16. What do you learn about His judgment?

4. How is His kingdom described in Isaiah 11:6-10?

5. What do you observe about knowledge in verse 9? How does this contrast with the condition of God's people described in Isaiah 5:13 and Hosea 4:6?

PROGRAM 26 | The Oracles to the Nations

TODAY'S TEXT
Isaiah 13:1-6

CROSS-REFERENCES
Isaiah 1:1; 2:2; 4; 6:1, 5-11; 7:1, 4, 9; 8:19-20; 9:6-7; 11:10; 14:28-29; 15:1; 17:1

Amos 3:7

Ephesians 4:14

1. What are the overall themes of chapters 1-6 and 7-12?

2. Today we will begin a new segment in Isaiah, chapters 13-23: "The Oracles to the Nations." Read chapter 13:1-6, marking key words including references to God's *anger* and time phrases.

3. Who does this first oracle concern? Mark references to this nation and its king in black, with a purple "B."

4. What do you learn about God's sovereign judgment in verses 2-3?

5. Cyrus the Great and Darius the Mede defeated the Babylonian Empire in 539 B.C. (though they did not destroy the city). Does this prophecy reach beyond this? What phrase helps you understand this?

6. Read 2 Thessalonians 1:7-9 and list what happens to those who don't know God and disobey His Gospel. What does this truth compel you to do?

PROGRAM 27 | The Day of His Burning Anger

TODAY'S TEXT
Isaiah 13:1, 4-16

CROSS-REFERENCES

Isaiah 1:2

Numbers 32:23

Psalm 51:5

Joel 2:1-12

Malachi 4:5-6

John 3:19

Romans 1:21-32

Revelation 11:3-8

1. Observe Isaiah 13:5-16, marking key words from your bookmark. Mark the **Lord, His anger,** and **destruction.** Add the day of the Lord to your list of key words and mark it with an orange box shaded pink. Look for geographical references like *world, earth,* and *land.*

   Suggestion: when you have a large list of key words, mark two or three at a time, asking the 5 Ws and H as you read. You don't want to miss the meaning of the passage. Repetitive reading will help you memorize the scriptures.

2. How will men react to the *day of the Lord?*

3. What kind of people face God's wrath? What happens to them?

4. Does this help you understand God's purpose for this day? What is it?

5. What did you learn about the Lord from this passage? What do you learn about His holiness, judgment on sin, sovereignty, etc.?

PROGRAM 28   "Babylon is fallen!"

Isaiah 13:8, 11, 13, 17-22

CROSS-REFERENCES

Malachi 4:5-6

Matthew 3:7

1 Thessalonians 5:1-2

2 Thessalonians 2:2-3

1 Peter 1:16

Revelation 17:1-6, 15-18; 18:4-5, 8, 10, 20, 23

1. Review your Isaiah 13:1-16 observations and then read verses 17-22, marking key words. Who will God send against Babylon?

2. What will they do to Babylon's people? What do you learn about future generations?

3. Look up the following verses and note what you learn about the day to come.

   a. 1 Thessalonians 5:1-3

   b. 2 Thessalonians 2:3

4. How can you apply these prophecies and warnings to your life? What do you have to know to stand firm?

PROGRAM 29   Life After Death

TODAY'S TEXT
Isaiah 14:1-16
CROSS-REFERENCES

Isaiah 2:22

Numbers 32:23

Psalm 119:104

Mark 9:44

Luke 16:26

John 14:6; 16:8-9

Romans 1:11

2 Corinthians 5:21

2 Peter 1:21

Revelation 17:4-6; 18:2; 20:12-11

1. Observe Isaiah 14:1-16 and mark references to **Babylon** and its king. Look carefully for time phrases and geographical locations. If the land refers to Israel (Canaan or land of the Lord), double underline it in green and shade it blue.

2. What do you learn about the Lord in verses 1-5? What will He do for Israel and to Babylon?

3. What will Israel do to the peoples in their midst (v.2)?

4. Mark references to **Sheol** (the transliterated Hebrew; hell and hades in other versions) with a red S in verses 11-15. What is it like, where is it, and who is there?

5. What do the kings of other nations say to Babylon's king?

PROGRAM 30

Who Can Turn Back His Hand?

TODAY'S TEXT
Isaiah 14:12-27

CROSS-REFERENCES

Isaiah 13:2

Genesis 11:1-9

Numbers 32:23

Psalm 139:9; 11

Jeremiah 50:1-3; 51:53

Luke 16:19-31; 23:42-43

1 Corinthians 15:20

2 Corinthians 5:8

Colossians 1:18

Revelation 20:7-14

1. Read Isaiah 14:1-15 for context and then observe verses 16-27, marking key words including references to Babylon and its king, time phrases, and geographical locations.

2. Describe the king of Babylon's descent. How far did he fall?

3. What will the Lord do to Babylon's people and land, according to verses 22-23?

4. What attribute of God is described in Isaiah 14:24-27?

5. What does this teach you about His plan for your life? Can circumstances, people, or even sin stop His plan for you?

PROGRAM 31 — Refuge in the Lord

TODAY'S TEXT
Isaiah 14:28-32

CROSS-REFERENCES
Isaiah 2:1-3; 6:1; 8:4
Exodus 7:10-12
1 Samuel 4:1; 5:1-4
Psalm 30:5
John 16:33

1. Observe Isaiah 14:28-32, marking time phrases with a green clock and God in yellow. Mark *crying* (*wail, mourn*) with a blue teardrop.

2. Who does this oracle concern and when did it occur?

3. What does God warn Philistia of in verse 29?

4. What will He do for the "helpless" and "needy" in Israel? Think about what brought them to this state.

5. What two things will God use to judge Philistia?

PROGRAM 32 — His Dwelling Place

TODAY'S TEXT
Isaiah 14:29, 32

CROSS-REFERENCES
Leviticus 25:2, 23
Deuteronomy 12:5
2 Samuel 5:7
2 Chronicles 6:5-6, 10, 24-25, 28-31; 7:14
Psalms 2:1-6, 10-12; 18:2; 30:5; 46:1
Proverbs 18:10
2 Peter 1:19
Revelation 5:10; 13:8; 21:2, 4

1. Review Isaiah 14:28-32. What do you learn about Zion (Jerusalem)?

2. In Leviticus 25 the Lord gives Moses the statutes concerning the land of Israel. What do you learn about the land in verse 23? Who owns it?

3. Look up Deuteronomy 12:5 (verses 1-11 for context). Where will God establish His name? What will the people do there?

4. Finally, read Psalm 2. Note what the text says about Zion, the nations, and God's warnings in verses 10-12.

5. "How blessed are all who take refuge in Him!" (Psalm 2:12) Are you seeking God in the midst of your trials? Are you resting in His promises to be your help, strength, and shield?

PROGRAM 33 | A Prideful Nation's Ruin

TODAY'S TEXT
Isaiah 15:1-9; 16:1-5

CROSS-REFERENCES

Genesis 12:3; 19:24-26, 37-38

Psalm 9:11-14; 30:5; 48:1-3, 8

Jonah 3:5

Zechariah 8:2-3, 6-8

1. Observe Isaiah 15:1-9 and 16:1-5. Mark key words, especially references to *wailing (crying)* with a blue teardrop.

2. What country does God address this oracle to and what has happened to it?

3. Why are the people crying? Note who is wailing and other descriptions of their grief. Also find out where they go to weep.

4. What will God to this nation according to verse 9?

5. What is the instruction to this nation in 16:1?

6. What kind of ruler will one day reign over the people in Zion? Why does the Lord place this Messianic promise in the oracle to Moab?

PROGRAM 34 | God Opposes the Proud

TODAY'S TEXT
Isaiah 15:1-9; 16:1-5

CROSS-REFERENCES

Isaiah 14:13-15

Genesis 3:5; 19:30-38

1. Re-read Isaiah 15:1-9 and 16:1-5 for context. Then observe Isaiah 16:6-14, marking *wail* with a blue teardrop, *pride* with a red arrow pointing up, and *therefore.*

2. Describe Moab's pride?

3. What will happen to them? What will their enemies do to the land?

4. What do you learn about God from these verses? Especially note what He says in verses 9-10.

5. Who does Moab turn to in their crisis according to verse 12? How does this contrast with the refuge they could receive from Israel (16:3-5)?

PROGRAM 35   Men and the Maker

TODAY'S TEXT
Isaiah 17:1-14; 18:1-7

CROSS-REFERENCES
Isaiah 7:4, 9; 14:29-32; 15:1

Psalm 30:5

Proverbs 18:10

Hosea 4:6

Matthew 25:31

Colossians 3:5

1 Peter 4:17

1. Read Isaiah 17 and 18 slowly, paying attention to the vivid imagery in this oracle. Mark time phrases with a green clock and identify the different nations.

2. Who's facing judgment in verses 1-3 and who are they compared to in verse 3? What happens?

3. Who does the subject shift to in verse 4? What will happen to them and their land?

4. What will God's judgment cause the people to do according to verse 7?

5. What do you learn about their behavior from verses 9-11? What will they suffer, according to verse 11?

6. What do you learn about the people of Cush in 18:1-2?

7. Do you flirt with idols that bring on God's wrath (Colossians 3:5-6)?

PROGRAM 36 — God's Purpose for the Nations

TODAY'S TEXT
Isaiah 19:1-4, 12, 17

CROSS-REFERENCES

Isaiah 14:24-27

Esther 4:14

Daniel 4:35

1 Corinthians 15:58

1. Observe Isaiah 19:1-4, 12 and 17 watching for what God does. Who does the oracle concern?

2. Who do the Egyptians worship according to verse 1?

3. What will the Lord cause to happen (v. 2)?

4. Who will the Egyptians turn to as their society crumbles? How does this compare to modern countries in times of hardship?

5. Who will God appoint to rule over them?

6. If God has a purpose and is sovereign over the world, what can you conclude about your nation's current events? About your circumstances?

PROGRAM 37 — His Powerful Purpose

TODAY'S TEXT
Isaiah 19:1-25

CROSS-REFERENCES

Isaiah 14:24

1 Chronicles 12:32

Jeremiah 17:14

Daniel 11:36, 40-43

2 Corinthians 10:5

1 Timothy 2:2

1. Read Isaiah 19 and color references to the *Lord* in yellow. Mark the time phrase *in that day* in a distinct way. Also mark *purpose(d)* with a squiggly line.

2. Review your observations on verses 1-4 from the last program—God's judgment on Egypt. How will this judgment impact daily life in Egypt according to verses 5-10?

3. What do you learn about Egypt's leaders in verses 11-15? (Remember Egypt is historically renowned for its advanced technology and philosophies.) What has the Lord done to them and how has their leadership affected the people?

4. In verses 16-25 the phrase *in that day* is used six times. How are the Egyptians described in verse 16 and what has brought them to this state? Who will they dread and why? What else will happen "in that day" according to verse 18? Contrast the state of Egypt in verses 19-20 and verse 3. What have they built and where? Who will they turn to in their demoralized state this time? Who is their oppressor and who will deliver them? What do you learn from verses 21 and 22 about the Egyptians and the Lord? How do you know their vows to the Lord are genuine? As a result of the Egyptian's faith in the Lord, what will happen in that region of the world according to verses 23-25?

5. What was God's purpose for judging Egypt? Was their suffering in vain? What will He accomplish?

6. The Lord used a decaying society, failing government, declining economy, and oppressive regime to draw Egypt to Himself. What is He using in your life to draw you close? Who is your Deliverer?

PROGRAM 38 | "I Am God... There Is No Other"

TODAY'S TEXT
Isaiah 20:1-6; 21:1-5

CROSS-REFERENCES

Isaiah 14:24, 28;
19:22; 45:5-7

Jeremiah 29:11

Amos 3:6-7

Romans 8:28

2 Corinthians 3:18;
4:17-18

1. Observe Isaiah 20, marking key words and time phrases; mark *sign* with an orange stop sign. Ask 5 W and H questions: who is this prophecy about, when was it given, what is going to happen, etc.

2. What did the Lord tell Isaiah to do? Why?

3. Who will be "dismayed and ashamed"?

4. Why were God's people putting their hope in these nations?

5. What is God teaching Israel? What is He showing you in these passages? Can deliverance be found apart from God?

PROGRAM 39 | Depend On Him!

TODAY'S TEXT
Isaiah 21:1-17; 22:1-13

CROSS-REFERENCES

Isaiah 14:24, 27; 36:12;
57:1

2 Chronicles 32:8

Psalms 119:38; 139:16

Ecclesiastes 3:7

Jeremiah 23:16

Joel 3:14

Matthew 7:6

Luke 15:4

John 18:9; 17:12

2 Corinthians 5:8

1. Observe Isaiah 21:1-17 and 22:1-13. Mark key words including *destruction* with red flames and time phrases with a green clock. Note in the margins what God addresses in each oracle and its location on your map. Also, review your observations of Isaiah 21:1-5 from the previous program.

2. What does the lookout report in the first oracle in chapter 21? Why is this sobering news to Israel?

3. Summarize the main points of the oracle to Edom.

4. What do you learn about the people of Arabia? How quickly will their judgment take place?

5. Spend some time examining your life. Ask yourself who you depend on when things are good and bad. Then commit to live in total surrender to God's will.

PROGRAM 40 | Temporal or Eternal?

TODAY'S TEXT
Isaiah 22:4-25; 23:1-18

CROSS-REFERENCES
Isaiah 14:24, 28; 26:4; 37:12; 46:11

Genesis 21:33

2 Chronicles 32:7-9

Psalm 90:1-3; 93:2

Ezekiel 27:36

Joel 2

Romans 8:28

2 Corinthians 4:18; 5:1-3

James 4:6

Revelation 3:8

1. Read Isaiah 22 and 23—the final oracles to the nations. Mark key words and time phrases as you have previously and ask the 5 W and H questions as you read.

2. Isaiah 22:12 begins with "therefore." Why does the Lord call His people to wail? Review the previous verses for context.

3. How do they behave instead? What does the Lord say then?

4. What do you learn about Tyre's reputation, livelihood, origin, benefactors, etc. from 23:1-8?

5. Why will the Lord judge Tyre? How?

PROGRAM 41 — A Day of Reckoning

TODAY'S TEXT
Isaiah 24:1-6

CROSS-REFERENCES

Isaiah 14:24; 5:20

Genesis 9:16

1 Corinthians 6:11

1 Thessalonians 4:1-6

2 Peter 3:3-4

1. Carefully read Isaiah 24:1-6. What will the Lord do to the earth and its people?

2. How are the people described in verse 2? What does this mean?

3. What do you learn about the earth from verses 3-4?

4. Who fades away? What does the repetition of this topic in Isaiah tell you about God?

5. How will you respond to this knowledge? Are you of the world, denying a day of wrath and judgment, or of the faithful remnant, living in ways that please God?

PROGRAM 42 — Man's Corruption, the Earth's Pollution

TODAY'S TEXT
Isaiah 24:1-6

CROSS-REFERENCES

Isaiah 24:21

Genesis 1:1-4, 22, 26-27; 2:8, 16-17; 3:1-6, 24; 4:8-16; 6:1-3, 5-8, 11-14, 18; 9:1, 5, 9, 12-14, 16-17; 15:17-18

Matthew 24:38

Romans 5:12

Philippians 2:15-16

2 Timothy 4:1-4

1. Review Isaiah 24:1-6 and mark *covenant* in red with a yellow box. Also double underline *earth* in green (a geographical location) and shade it brown.

2. What three things are the inhabitants of the earth guilty of doing? Put a number by each in verse 5.

3. Let's establish some context to understand God's creation, His purpose for it, and how man violated God's "everlasting covenant." Read the following verses and note what you learn about God, man, and covenant.
   a. Creation – Genesis 1
   b. God's command to Adam – 2:16-17
   c. Adam and Eve's sin – 3:6
   d. Cain's sin – 4:9-16
   e. Noah and the Flood – 6:1-8, 11-18
   f. The Everlasting Covenant – 9:5-17

4. What happens to the earth when society doesn't execute justice? How does this help you understand why God will judge the earth?

5. In light of your study today, evaluate the command in 2 Timothy 4:1-4. What is your responsibility? Are you prepared to fulfill it? What is the urgency?

PROGRAM 43 — "It Will Fall, Never To Rise Again"

TODAY'S TEXT
Isaiah 24:1-21

CROSS-REFERENCES

Genesis 9:5-6

Haggai 2:3, 6-7

Romans 2:11

Philippians 2:15

Hebrews 12:25-29

2 Peter 3:3-4, 7, 9, 18

Revelation 6:10; 11:15-18; 16:18, 21

1. Observe Isaiah 24 and continue marking *earth* and its pronouns. Also watch for time phrases like *in that day, then, after many days,* etc., which indicate event order.

2. Verse 6 says few men are left. How is life for them described in verses 7-13?

3. What does the analogy in verse 13 help you understand

4. What else do you learn about the survivors in verses 17-18? Can anyone escape?

5. What is your response to today's study? Awe? Fear? If the Lord comes in your lifetime, will you be among the faithful remnant crying out "Glory to the Righteous One"?

PROGRAM 44 — Judgment for the Host of Heaven

TODAY'S TEXT
Isaiah 24:21-23

CROSS-REFERENCES

Genesis 6:1-2; 9:5

Deuteronomy 32:4

Job 1:6

Matthew 25:41

Mark 9:48

2 Corinthians 5:21

Ephesians 3:17; 6:12

2 Peter 2:2-4, 8-9

Jude 1:6

Revelation 12:7-12; 20:1-8, 10-15

1. Review Isaiah 24:21-23. Who will God punish? What will He do?

2. Look up "host of heaven" in Revelation 12:7-12.
   a. Who's at war?
   b. What's the immediate outcome?
   c. What happens afterward on earth?

3. Now read Revelation 20:1-7. Mark references to the *devil* with a red pitchfork and *thousand years* with a clock.
   a. What do you learn about Satan?
   b. Where does he spend a thousand years?
   c. Does this bear on the interpretation of Isaiah 24:21-23?

4. Carefully read John 3:16-18 and 2 Corinthians 5:21. What is God's solution to man's dilemma?

PROGRAM 45 — Victory in Jesus!

TODAY'S TEXT
Isaiah 24:21-23; 25:1-12

CROSS-REFERENCES
Isaiah 14:26; 24:1, 6

Mark 9:46

John 15:14, 18

Romans 6:23

1 Corinthians 15:42, 51-54, 56-58

2 Corinthians 4:4

Philippians 2:15

2 Peter 3:10

Revelation 20:15; 21:1-8, 22-23; 22:1-7, 12, 17

1. Read Isaiah 24:21-23 and 25:1-12. Mark time phrases and circle the phrase *He will swallow up death for all time.* Also double underline in green references to the *mountain* (Jerusalem) and shade them blue. Describe the subject shift from chapter 24 to 25.

2. What will follow God's judgment of "the host of heaven" and "the kings of the earth"?

3. Why does Isaiah praise God in 25:1-5? What do you learn about God's character from these verses? What does he compare God to?

4. What will God do for His people according to verses 6-8? How will they respond? Meditate on the majesty and wonder of this day.

5. Look at the final verses in Isaiah 25. How does the fate of these people contrast with the destiny of God's people?

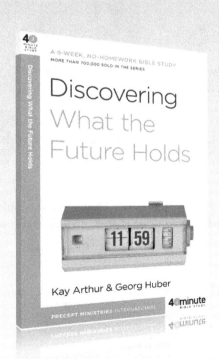

PROGRAM 46 | **Peace in Turmoil**

TODAY'S TEXT
Isaiah 26:1-4

CROSS-REFERENCES

Isaiah 1:4, 7-9, 18; 2:2-4, 6-8; 5:1-2, 13-26; 6:1-3, 5, 7-9, 13; 7:2-4, 9, 14; 9:6; 11:1; 14:24; 19:23; 24:1, 5-6, 23; 26: 7, 19; 27:13

1 Timothy 6:15

Romans 7:18; 8:28

1. Review the previous chapters in this segment—Isaiah 24 and 25. What event is detailed? Why does it occur? What happens to the earth's inhabitants? To God's people?

2. Now read Isaiah 26:1-4, marking time phrases. What happens *in that day?*

3. Who will receive peace? How?

4. What is God called that tells us we can fully trust Him?

PROGRAM 47 | **The Heavenly City**

TODAY'S TEXT
Isaiah 26:1-9

CROSS-REFERENCES

Isaiah 1:2; 2:17; 11:16; 24:3-4; 25:9

Genesis 3:1, 5

Deuteronomy 31:30; 32:1-4

Hebrews 11:6, 13-14, 16

1. Observe Isaiah 26:1-9, marking *righteous(ness)* and **peace.** What do the righteous enter? How is "the righteous nation" described?

2. What do you learn about God from these verses? Compare this passage with Moses' song in Deuteronomy 32:1-4.

3. Now look up Hebrews 11:13-16 (read 1-12 for context). How are the people described in these verses? What has God prepared for them? How does this relate to Isaiah 26:1-2?

4. Contrast the "strong city" in Isaiah 26:1 with the "unassailable city" in verses 5-6. What will God do to this proud people?

5. What do you learn about the *righteous* in verse 7? How does God enable His people to stand firm and follow Him in adversity and difficult times?

PROGRAM 48 | Persevering Through Trials

TODAY'S TEXT
Isaiah 26:7-16

CROSS-REFERENCES
Isaiah 26:3, 5
Job 36:30-32; 37:10-12
Psalm 119:67, 71; 148:8
Jeremiah 14:1, 22
Amos 3:6
Matthew 17:17-20
John 5:19
Romans 2:4
Philippians 2:13
Hebrews 10:32-38; 11:10

1. Observe Isaiah 26:7-16, then re-read verse 7. What does God do for the righteous?

2. Read Hebrews 10:32-39. What have the readers endured? How does the writer encourage them to press on? How should they live?

3. How are the wicked and righteous contrasted in Isaiah 26:9-12? Consider who God softened and hardened by His judgments.

4. What did you learn about God's sovereignty from these verses in Isaiah?

5. What truths from today's study can you apply to your life?

PROGRAM 49 | Surpassing Peace for the Righteous

TODAY'S TEXT
Isaiah 26:12-21

CROSS-REFERENCES
Genesis 7:1, 16
Exodus 12
Numbers 35:33
Psalm 119:71
Daniel 12:2
Zechariah 4:6
John 1:1; 3:16; 5:24-30; 14:10
2 Corinthians 5:21
Revelation 3:10

1. Observe Isaiah 26:12-21, asking the 5W and Hs. Continue marking *earth, peace, God,* and the *righteous* including synonyms and pronouns.

2. What did you learn about God from these verses? What does He do for His people?

3. Study the description of God's people in verses 16-18. What are they *not* able to do?

4. What does God command His people in Isaiah 26:20? For how long?

5. What will the Lord do to the inhabitants of the earth according to verse 21? Relate this to Numbers 35:33.

| PROGRAM 50 | **The Serpent's Destiny** |

TODAY'S TEXT
Isaiah 27:1-13

CROSS-REFERENCES

Isaiah 5:1-2; 11:11-12, 16; 24:1, 21; 26:1, 20-21

Genesis 3:5

Deuteronomy 4:27

2 Corinthians 5:8

Ephesians 2:2; 6:13, 17

1 Thessalonians 4:16-17

Revelation 12:9-12; 13:1, 3-4; 19:11-15, 19-20; 20:1-3, 7-10

1. Review Isaiah 24:21, noting who God judges. Then read Isaiah 26:20-21 and 27:1 marking *in that day.* According to these verses, who does God punish?

2. How is Leviathan described? List your observations.

3. Now look up Genesis 3:1, 5, Revelation 12:9, and 13:1, 3-4. What do you learn about the serpent (dragon)? How is his power described? Who worships him?

4. Read Revelation 19:11-15, 19-20, and 20:1-3. What happens to the serpent and those who follow him? Who executes God's judgment? How?

5. Lastly, examine Revelation 20:7-10. What is the serpent's destiny?

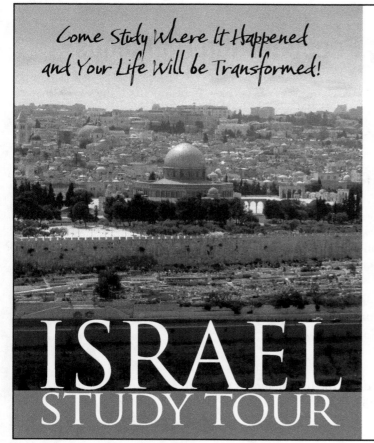

| PROGRAM 51 | **Understanding Your Enemies** |

TODAY'S TEXT
Isaiah 31:1

CROSS-REFERENCES
Isaiah 28:16; 64:8
Genesis 3:19
Jeremiah 13:11
Acts 20:27
Titus 1:1; 2:5

1. As we begin a new segment in Isaiah, read Isaiah 28–33 to get an overview. Mark the six *woes* and ask 5W and H questions as you observe them.

2. Locate the nations mentioned in these chapters on your map and note their proximities to Israel.

3. Briefly describe who and what the people of Israel relied on rather than God.

4. How does the spiritual condition of Israel at this time compare to your nation's? To yours?

| PROGRAM 52 | **Getting the Big Picture** |

TODAY'S TEXT
Isaiah 28-33

CROSS-REFERENCES
Isaiah 1:1; 5:13; 6:1;
7:1-4, 7, 9; 9:6; 14:24,
27-28; 24:1 26:3; 28:16;
29:1, 16; 30:15; 64:8
Proverbs 29:25
John 6:37; 14:6
1 Peter 2:6

1. Today we will review the major segments of Isaiah covered so far in our study. Learning how each segment fits into the book helps us more accurately understand the book's overall theme. Begin by noting the following segment divisions:
   a. Chapters 1-12   c. Chapters 24-27
   b. Chapters 13-23   d. Chapters 28-33

2. In the first segment, God primarily addresses Judah (Southern Kingdom) though He sometimes refers to Ephraim (Northern Kingdom).
   a. Review some of the key verses from this segment: Isaiah 1:2-4, 5:13, and 7:9.
   b. What have God's chosen people done to Him?
   c. What will happen to them?

3. The second segment contains oracles against surrounding nations.
   a. Review the nations God addresses and their relationships to Israel.
   b. Look up Isaiah 14:24, 27. What is God's message of hope amid these prophecies of destruction?

4. In the third segment, God addresses all inhabitants of the earth.
   a. Review Isaiah 24:1, 5, and 21 to learn what will happen.
   b. How does God assure the faithful remnant in 26:3?

5. The fourth segment is directed at Israel. Study key verse Isaiah 30:15 and commit it to memory. Meditate on its truth and think about how you can apply it to your daily walk.

PROGRAM 53 — Pride's Deadly Consequences

TODAY'S TEXT
Isaiah 28:1-13

CROSS-REFERENCES

2 Chronicles 16:9

Amos 6:1, 4-9

John 8:32

Ephesians 1:14

2 Peter 1:3

1. Observe Isaiah 28:1-13 with 5W and H questions. Mark *woe* with a red cloud shaded brown and *pride* with a red arrow pointing up (include synonyms). Also mark key words from your bookmark.

2. What did you learn from marking *woe?* Who is it addressed to and why?

3. Who will humble the proud kingdom and how? Describe His agent of judgment. What does the text say about when this will occur?

4. What have God's people rejected according to verse 12?

5. Read Ephesians 4:14. What are the consequences of following unsound, ungodly teachers? Who are you putting your trust in?

PROGRAM 54 — Resisting Insults

TODAY'S TEXT
Isaiah 28:14-29

CROSS-REFERENCES

Isaiah 1:1; 9:6; 11:1; 16:5; 24:1; 26:3

Joshua 10:12

2 Samuel 5:20

Psalm 1:1-2

John 1:11-12; 14:6

Acts 20:27

1 Corinthians 15:58

1 Peter 2:4-7

2 Peter 3:3-6

1. Re-read Isaiah 28:1-13 for context and then observe verses 14-29, marking key words. Who is the Lord talking to in these verses? What is their status in Jerusalem?

2. *Pride* is a key word in Isaiah. In what ways are these "scoffers" arrogant? What do they believe according to verse 15?

3. What will God do?

4. What is the "cornerstone" in verse 16? Look up 1 Peter 2:4-7.

5. "The fear of the Lord is the beginning of wisdom" (Psalm 111:10). What wisdom can you glean from Psalm 1:1-2? Evaluate these verses in light of your study today.

PROGRAM 55 | The City of God

TODAY'S TEXT
Isaiah 29:1-24

CROSS-REFERENCES

2 Chronicles 36:15-17, 20

Zechariah 14:2-3, 9

Malachi 4:2

Matthew 24:15-16, 21, 23, 27, 30

Luke 21:20-24

Philippians 2:10-11

1. Read Isaiah 29, marking key words, time phrases, and geographical locations. Note especially the two woes and who they concern. Also watch for truths about God.

2. According to verses 1-4, what will God do to Ariel (Jerusalem)? Describe this judgment.

3. Isaiah 29:5 begins with "but," introducing a contrast. Who is Israel delivered from and when? Who delivers the nation and how?

4. Why is the Lord going to judge Jerusalem?

   a. What do verses 1, 9-14 reveal about the people? Why are they ignorant of God's plans?

   b. What do verses 15-16 show about the hearts of the leaders?

5. Verses 17-24 call God's remnant to look ahead. What does He promise? How does He address rulers at this time? What will Jerusalem be like?

Get Trained!

Learn how to study like Kay and the team at *Precepts for Life*™. Get trained in the tools of the Inductive Bible Study Method. Unlock even more of the power of God's Word for yourself.

You can even be trained to lead a local Bible study at your church and in your community.

For current courses and a schedule of upcoming training in Chattanooga or in a city near you, TV viewers call 1.800.763.1990, radio listeners call 1.888.734.7707, or visit www.PreceptsForLife. com and click the "Workshops and Classes" tab.

PROGRAM 56 — Blessed Are Those Who Long For Him

TODAY'S TEXT
Isaiah 30:1-2, 18

CROSS-REFERENCES

Isaiah 1:2, 4, 18; 7:4, 7, 9; 20:1-4; 26:3; 30:1-2, 18; 31:1

Psalm 119:104

Matthew 6:33

1. Observe Isaiah 30:1-2, 18, marking *woe* with a red cloud, shaded brown. Who is God talking to in these verses?

2. According to verse 1, what have they done?

3. Who do they trust for deliverance rather than God? (Cf. Isaiah 31:1.)

4. How did King Ahaz exemplify the behavior of this rebellious people? What did God tell him in Isaiah 7:9? What path did he choose?

5. Meditate on the truths from today's programs. Do you wait on the Lord, trusting His plans?

PROGRAM 57 — Beware False Teachers

TODAY'S TEXT
Isaiah 30:1-15, 18

CROSS-REFERENCES

Isaiah 6:9-13

Matthew 5:17-18

John 12:48

Philippians 1:29

2 Timothy 1:1; 3:1-5, 13-16; 4:1-3

1. Read Isaiah 30:1-15 marking key words from your bookmark. What happens to "rebellious children" who ally with Egypt? Describe the alliance.

2. What are they doing with their wealth according to verse 6? Will their treacherous journey be worth it? Read 2 Kings 18:13-16 for additional context.

3. What does God command Isaiah to write? Why?

4. Compare verses 9-11 with Isaiah 1:4; 6:9-10 and Jeremiah 14:14. What do you learn about the faith of these people? What do they *want* to hear? Why?

5. Have you succumbed to teachers who tell you you're *entitled* to health and wealth and can actually *claim* them from God? Whose will do you want?

PROGRAM 58 — Looking to the Arm of Flesh

TODAY'S TEXT
Isaiah 30:15-26

CROSS-REFERENCES

Isaiah 1:5-6, 18; 2:4; 32:1

Exodus 32:3-4, 9; 33:2-3, 12-15, 20-23; 34:5

Psalm 139:16

Proverbs 18:10-12

Jeremiah 29:11; 30:11

John 16:33

Romans 8:28

1. Review Isaiah 30:1-15 for context, and then observe verses 15-26. Mark *therefore* with three red dots like a triangle and note the conclusions.

2. Who is Judah looking to for aid and protection against the Assyrians? What does God say about this country? What will happen?

3. What does He want His people to do according to verse 15? How do they respond?

4. How will they be humiliated by the enemy?

5. In verse 26 God says He will heal the bruise He inflicted. What can you conclude from this chapter about His purpose in bruising us? Are bruises a *final* product?

PROGRAM 59 — God's Compassion for the Repentant

TODAY'S TEXT
Isaiah 30:27-33; 31:1-9; 32:1-4

CROSS-REFERENCES

Isaiah 6:8-10; 30:1, 15, 18

Zechariah 14:2-4

Matthew 3:1-3; 4:17

John 4:23

Colossians 3:5

Hebrews 13:8

Revelation 19:15-16

1. Review Isaiah 30:18-26, then read verses 27-33 noting everything you learn about the Lord. Mark *hearing, listening* with a green ear and *anger* as you did previously.

2. What attributes of God do you see in this passage?

3. What will happen to Israel's enemies? How does God execute His judgment?

4. Now read Isaiah 31. How does this chapter parallel chapter 30? List similarities you observe about Egypt, God's restoration of Israel and His judgment on their enemies.

5. Have you, like Israel, "defected" from the Lord? What does God want you to do about it? Are *you* willing to do it?

PROGRAM 60 | Cast Off Complacency

TODAY'S TEXT
Isaiah 32:3, 5-20

CROSS-REFERENCES

Isaiah 22:13; 30:13, 15, 18; 31:9; 40:3; 55:1

Judges 5:6-7

Psalms 25; 27:11-14; 62:1-2, 6-8

Ezekiel 36:27-29

1. Observe Isaiah 32. Mark **hear (ear), righteousness,** and **wait** in distinctive ways with other key words, time phrases, and geographical locations. Watch for changes in verb tense and determine if texts are specifying near or far future events.

2. When do verses 1-8 occur? How is this time described?

3. What do you learn about the fool, rogue, and nobleman? Do these descriptions compare to anyone you know? What about you?

4. What will it be like after the Spirit is poured out? When will this occur?

5. Are you ready to take action—to stand in the gap for this generation, society, country? Are you boldly speaking truth and interceding on their behalf? Does your lifestyle proclaim God's standards?

PROGRAM 61 — The Lord is My Treasure

TODAY'S TEXT
Isaiah 33:1-2, 6, 17-19

CROSS-REFERENCES

Genesis 9:6, 9

Psalm 111:10

Matthew 24:12

Luke 21:28

Romans 1:19-20, 28-32

Ephesians 2:2-3

2 Timothy 3:1-5

1. As we prepare to observe Isaiah 33-35 this week, begin by meditating on key verse Isaiah 33:6. What is God to those who know Him?

2. Now think about today's headlines. What do they say about terror, radical religious groups, brutal regimes? Have they personally impacted your life? Are you afraid or resting in God's promises?

3. Look up 2 Timothy 3:1-5. What will man's character be like in the last days? Does this accurately describe people today?

4. Go back to Isaiah 33 and observe verses 1-2, 17-19. What does God say about the treacherous?

5. What does the remnant pray in verse 2? How will they endure the treacherous? What insight does this give you about living today?

PROGRAM 62 — Hope for the Hopeless

TODAY'S TEXT
Isaiah 33:1-17

CROSS-REFERENCES

Isaiah 6:3; 9:6-7; 22:13; 26:3; 34:8; 40:1

Deuteronomy 32:39

Jeremiah 1:12; 6:14

Philippians 1:28

Hebrews 12:29

1. Observe Isaiah 33:1-17. Mark the key word *woe.* What enemy was dealing treacherously with Israel? Do you think verse 1 is general or applies only to this specific history? Explain your answer.

2. Verse 2 begins the remnant's prayer. What do they ask for? What do they acknowledge about the Lord?

3. Compare their prayer to what Paul says in Philippians 1:28. How should we face our spiritual opponents?

4. Read Jeremiah 1:12 and Isaiah 26:3. How do these verses comfort us in times of uncertainty?

PROGRAM 63

The Judge, The Lawgiver, The King

TODAY'S TEXT
Isaiah 33:17-24; 34:1-8

CROSS-REFERENCES

Isaiah 9:6-7; 32:1; 33:1, 6; 43:15

Genesis 12:1-3

1 Chronicles 21:22

Matthew 6:9-10

Acts 17:28

Revelation 2:21; 5:9; 14:18-20

1. Observe Isaiah 33:17-24. Ask the 5Ws and H to learn about Jerusalem (Zion) and the Lord in this passage.

2. Who is "the King" in verse 17? Look at the following verses for expanded descriptions:

    a. Isaiah 9:6-7
    b. Isaiah 32:1
    c. Isaiah 33:22
    d. Isaiah 43:15

3. Will peace ever come to Israel? Will it be free from terror and threats? List details the text gives you about the nation's status once the King begins His reign.

4. Now read Isaiah 34:1-8. What does God say to the nations?

5. Isaiah 34 clearly states that only the righteous will see the King. Who is *your* king? Who or what rules *your* life?

PROGRAM 64

Edom's Example

TODAY'S TEXT
Isaiah 34:6-17

CROSS-REFERENCES

Isaiah 5:13; 6:13; 24:1, 23; 33:6

Genesis 12:2-3; 25:19, 22-34

Leviticus 3:3-4

Psalm 119:104

Acts 20:27

Romans 1:20

2 Corinthians 5:21; 12:9

Hebrews 12:15-17

1 John 2:2

1. Observe Isaiah 34:6-17. Mark *Edom* and its pronouns in red, then double underline it in green. Also mark geographical locations and time phrases such as *forever and ever.* Locate Edom on your map.

2. How is God's judgment on Edom described? For whose sake does He judge according to verse 8?

3. What happens to the land? How long will it remain in this condition?

4. Who will possess Edom? For how long?

5. Isaiah 34:5 says the people of Edom were "devoted to destruction." Why is this nation an example to other nations? To you? How do you need to respond?

PROGRAM 65 | Marked for Eternity

TODAY'S TEXT
Isaiah 35:1-10

CROSS-REFERENCES
Isaiah 33:6
Genesis 12:1-3; 25:7-34
Leviticus 11:44
Numbers 20:14-21
Jeremiah 49:7-22
Ezekiel 35:3-15
Obadiah 1
Romans 3:23
2 Corinthians 5:21
Hebrews 12:14-17
1 Peter 1:7, 16
1 John 2:2

1. Review Isaiah 34 and your notes about Edom. Who did the Edomites descend from? What is his connection to Israel?

2. What's going to happen to Edom?

3. Now look up Genesis 12:1-3. What does God promise Abraham? Who will He curse?

4. Read Numbers 20:14-21, marking references to *Edom* including pronouns.
   a. What does Israel request?
   b. How does Edom respond?

5. Look up Jeremiah 49:16-22, Obadiah 1, and Ezekiel 35:3-15, marking references to *Edom* including pronouns and synonyms like Mount Seir and Bozrah as before.
   a. How do these passages compare with Isaiah 34?
   b. Why will God judge Edom? Be specific, and list the verses that answer.

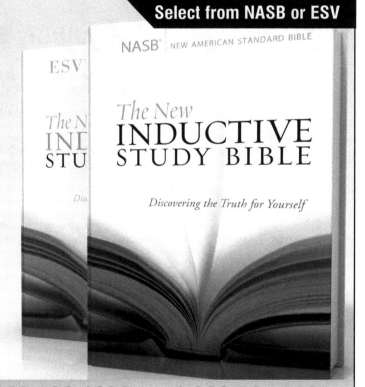

PROGRAM 66 | The Enemy's Challenge

TODAY'S TEXT
Isaiah 36:1-5

CROSS-REFERENCES

Isaiah 1:1, 9; 6:1, 5, 7-9, 13; 9:6; 7:1-3, 5-9, 11-14; 24:1, 5; 33:1, 17; 35:8, 10

2 Samuel 7:13-14

Romans 8:28

1. Observe Isaiah 36:1-5, marking time phrases and geographical locations. When does this chapter begin? What is happening?

2. Who comes to Jerusalem? Where does he meet Hezekiah's men?

3. How does the enemy challenge Hezekiah? What does he ask him?

4. How did Ahaz and Hezekiah react to their respective enemies? Who did they turn to? Compare 2 Kings 16:5, 7 with 2 Kings 19:1.

5. What is the spiritual value of being tested by enemies? How have you benefited from this experience?

PROGRAM 67 | The Enemy's Tactics

TODAY'S TEXT
Isaiah 36:2-11

CROSS-REFERENCES

Isaiah 31:1

1 Kings 13:18

2 Kings 18:1-4

2 Chronicles 30:1-2

Proverbs 7:16-19, 27

Matthew 4:3-7

Acts 20:27-32

Galatians 1:10

1. Begin your study today by looking at Hezekiah's character. Study 2 Kings 18:1-7 and 2 Chronicles 29:1-5, 10 and 30:1 to observe his relationship with the Lord and how he led God's people. List what you learn about him.

2. Now read Isaiah 36:2-11, carefully observing Rabshakeh's questions and statements. How does he try to weaken the people's confidence in Hezekiah? In God?

3. Why do you think Rabshakeh mentions the tearing down of the high places and altars to idols? Consider who's listening to his words (v. 11).

4. What "bargain" does he propose? Why would this deal be a compromise with the enemy?

5. How do Hezekiah's officials respond in verse 11? What's their concern?

6. Are you being tested? Are you tempted to compromise your loyalty to God? Who are you trusting in?

PROGRAM 68 — Resisting Compromise

TODAY'S TEXT
Isaiah 36:11-22; 37:1-10

CROSS-REFERENCES

Deuteronomy 33:27

Job 13:15

Psalms 56:3; 103:19

Proverbs 21:1; 29:25

Daniel 3:17-18

Joel 1:8, 13

Malachi 2:16

1 Corinthians 10:13; 12:26

2 Timothy 1:7

Hebrews 13:4

1. Review Isaiah 36:1-10, then read Isaiah 36:11-22 and 37:1-10. Continue to analyze the enemy's statements. Think about why he says what he does.

2. Why do Hezekiah's men ask Rabshakeh to speak Aramaic? What does Rabshakeh say? What is he trying to do?

3. What does Rabshakeh say about Hezekiah? What incentive does he offer them to betray their king?

4. How does the enemy try to marginalize the Lord? Who does he compare Him to?

5. How do Hezekiah and his men respond to the enemy's blasphemy?

6. How does God intervene? What does this teach you about God's character? Look up Psalm 103:19.

PROGRAM 69 — A Living Epistle to the World

TODAY'S TEXT
Isaiah 37:14-38; 38:1-6

CROSS-REFERENCES

Deuteronomy 32:39

2 Samuel 7:12-13

Psalm 31:15; 56:8; 139:2-3, 16

Jeremiah 13:11; 32:27

Zechariah 2:8

Romans 8:28-29

2 Corinthians 5:8

2 Timothy 4:10, 17

1 Peter 1:7

Revelation 2:9-11

1. Observe Isaiah 37:8-38, watching the order of events. Mark *remnant* and *pride* as you did before and also time phrases.

2. What is Rabshakeh's final message to Hezekiah? What does Hezekiah do with it?

3. Analyze Hezekiah's prayer in verses 14-20. What attributes of God does he believe in? Why does he ask for deliverance?

4. Why is God willing to respond favorably to Hezekiah's requests? List the verses that give you the answers.

5. Now read Isaiah 38:1-6—an event that occurred before Assyria attacked Jerusalem. What's wrong with Hezekiah? How does he respond to the news?

6. What does Isaiah say to him?

PROGRAM 70 — Hezekiah's Blessing

TODAY'S TEXT
Isaiah 38:1-22; 39:1-8

CROSS-REFERENCES
Numbers 6:24-25
2 Chronicles 32:24-26, 30-31
Romans 8:28
1 Corinthians 15:54
2 Corinthians 5:1, 8
Philippians 1:23; 3:10

1. Read Isaiah 38. What does verse 6 tell you about when these events occurred?

2. Now read 2 Kings 20 and 2 Chronicles 32:24-31. What additional details do you learn from these cross-references?

3. How did God respond to Hezekiah's prayer? What sign did He give?

4. Carefully re-read Hezekiah's record of his illness and recovery, and then answer the following questions.

   a. How did he feel about dying?

   b. What did he believe about God?

   c. What new perspective on life did he gain?

   d. How did his illness draw him closer to God?

Printed in the USA
CPSIA information can be obtained
at www.ICGtesting.com
LVHW071953140124
768898LV00080BA/2172

9 781621 190004